By   Anthony & David Morell

Terms and Conditions

LEGAL NOTICE

The Publisher has strived to be as accurate and complete as possible in the creation of this report, notwithstanding the fact that he does not warrant or represent at any time that the contents within are accurate due to the rapidly changing nature of the Internet.

While all attempts have been made to verify information provided in this publication, the Publisher assumes no responsibility for errors, omissions, or contrary interpretation of the subject Matter herein. Any perceived slights of specific persons, peoples, or organizations are unintentional.

In practical advice books, like anything else in life, there are no guarantees of income made. Readers are cautioned to reply on their own judgment about their individual circumstances to act accordingly.

This book is not intended for use as a source of legal, business, accounting or financial advice. All readers are advised to seek services of competent professionals in legal, business, accounting and finance fields.

You are encouraged to print this book for easy reading.

Table Of Contents

Foreword

Chapter 1:
What Is Network Marketing

Chapter 2:
How Important Is Your Site

Chapter 3:
How Important Is The Product

Chapter 4:
Finding Keywords

Chapter 5:
Paid Traffic

Chapter 6:
Free Traffic

Chapter 7:
Using Social Media

Chapter 8:
Assembling A Team

Chapter 9:
How Important Is Customer Service

Chapter 10:
The Mindset Necessary For Internet Marketing Success

Wrapping Up

Foreword

The idea of network marketing is sold as a tool to make money based on an individual's own sales as well as sales from those recruited by the individual. This is of course a very lucrative way of garnering income thus the enthusiasm to recruit as many people as possible to join in the business the better.

Network Marketers Manual
Grab The Most Powerful Network Marketing Tools And Strategies And Become The Next MLM Mogul

Chapter 1:

What Is Network Marketing

Synopsis

The network marketing requires the individual and the team under the direction of the individual to be able to sell products using the direct contact way of marketing. Some of these items sold do require the personal contact between the buyer and seller in order to ensure the product is happily bought.

The Basics

On the down side these network companies are frequently faced with problems like constant criticism, price fixing accusations, utilizing the pyramid schemes system, high initial start up costs and many others. There have also been cases where the companies are actually faced with law suits because of the sometimes rather questionable ethics and dealings.

However for those who are very outgoing and focused on making a career from this type of work, find it very rewarding indeed. For them the remunerations are worth the time and effort they put in. though it should be noted, that network marketing is not suitable for those individual who are not really committed or for those people who are shy.

Perhaps taking the relevant precautions to ensure the potential company one intends to join for network marketing is legal and sanctioned by the relevant authorities is very wise indeed. One should also be aware of the fundamentals of the company's policies so that there is not future misunderstandings and disappointments.

Training programs provided by the company is another important tool to enquire about. Without the supporting training it may be difficult to successfully sell the product in question.

Chapter 2:

How Important Is Your Site

Synopsis

Using the website to garner interest in a particular product is definitely the avenue to pursue in these current media savvy ear. Most people looking for or posting information do so now on the internet. Therefore although there are other more conventional ways of seeking information, by far the internet is the most popularly used source.

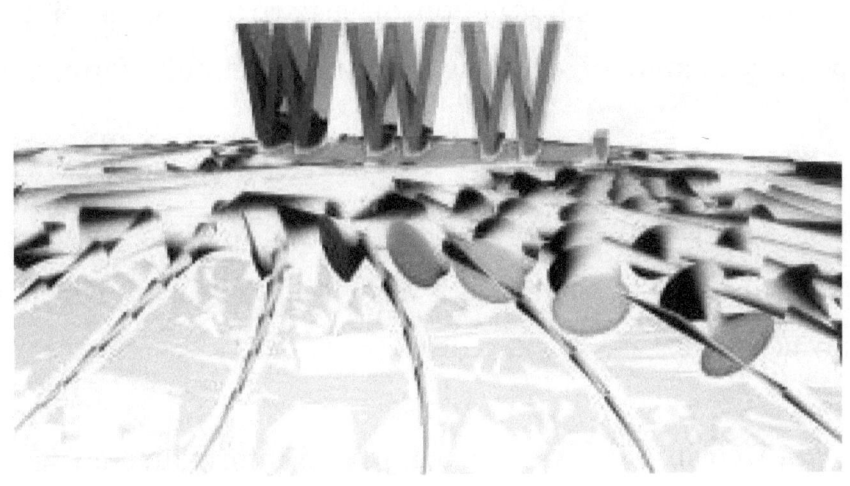

The Website

Website can be better and different yet more effective in being the mode on information exchange. This particular form of media exposure will ensure the "right" people are being directed to the products or services they are seeking.

However knowing the various techniques that should be used when hosting information on the website will be very beneficial in garnering traffic to the site.

Using key words in order to direct potential clients to a particular website is the only way the websites can be accessed continuously and consistently.

When time is of the essence, using the internet as a search tool will be the individual seeking information on a particular issue or item a huge possible amount of solutions and further helpful information.

When the key words are type in the search will begin and the individual's website will be pulled into the surfing zone, thus enticing the potential client to visit. This is very useful exposure which costs virtually nothing.

Creating a website that is eye catching and informative at the same time is very important if the idea is to hold the potential client's attention. Most people will not take the trouble to thoroughly run hrough a website if the initial few seconds spent on the website does not perk their interest. Therefore if one wants to host a website then the design and content should bear some serious thought. Colors and pictures are always a good attention drawing tool.

Chapter 3:
How Important Is The Product

Synopsis

Venturing into the network marketing world is always risky yet exciting and the remunerations are also quite good. Therefore to minimize the risks involved, one should try to do as must research into the intended foray as possible.

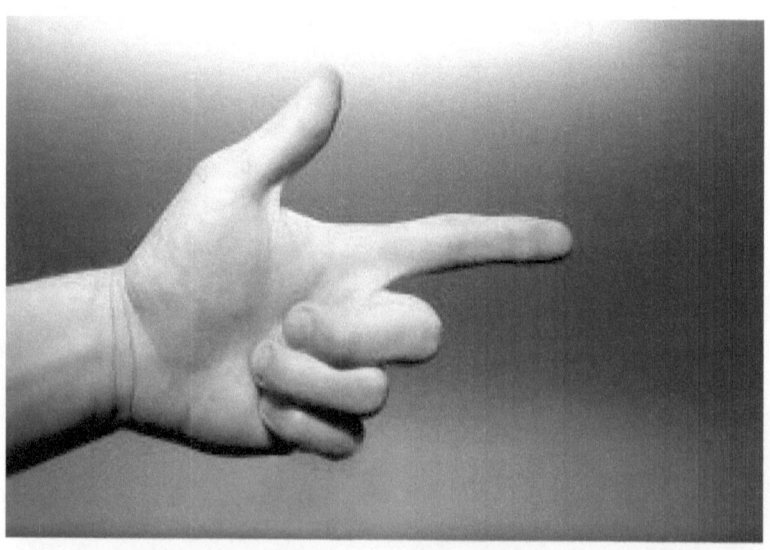

The Merchandise

One of the areas that need very careful consideration is in the product one decides to represent or promote with the intention of making it a business earning income. Choosing the right product will most certainly determine the success of the business venture to a certain extent.

If the item chosen is easily represented and accepted then half the battle is won. Now all the individual has to do, is to promote the item in a way that is so enticing that the customer will feel deprived if the item is not bought on the spot. This of course requires the savvy skills of a sales pitch and speaker.

Though good, if an item is on the rather expensive side, the chances of making a successful sale are also cut by fifty percent. It would be only natural to assume that the cost of the item is related to the added features incorporated in the said item, thus making is not only expensive but perhaps even to some extent to a real necessity for the average person.

This then adds to the fact that the customer base is now not only quite limited but perhaps also applicable to only a niche market, further shrinking the possible marketability of the chosen product.

Another point to consider when deciding on an above average priced product is the general economic environment of the times. If everyone is in the process of watching their current expenses, it is going to be even harder to conclude a sale successfully. Some may even consider the product to be a luxury rather than a necessity thus nullifying the sale.

Chapter 4:
Finding Keywords

Synopsis

Most people using the internet as a search engine would be likely to type in what they are looking for or any information connected to the item they are interested in.

If an individual was interested in hosting a website with the intention of creating a source of income from the said website then it would be necessary to ensure as much "traffic" as possible is directed to the website. The more traffic the website can garner the more the website can be profitable.

To Get Attention

Keywords are very important to ensure more traffic is directed to the site even though an individual is not looking for the particular item or information being promoted or posted. The idea is to bring the potential client or customer to the site and then try to keep the customer's or client's attention long enough to perk his or her interest.

The following are just some suggestions to consider when making the decision to ensure key words are used:

- Checking the competitor's key words will often enable the individual to be more aware of what the potential hits are looking for when surfing the net is done.
- Once the general idea and list of key words are noted then the individual can set about adding his or her own key words to the possible list that is going to be eventually used.
- Getting the help of others is also an advantage, after all more minds are better that just one. What may appear to the individual may not be appealing to others, thus the need for outside input.
- Being specific and to the point is also very important. Most people use the internet for the prime reason of time saving therefore going "round the bush" to say something that could be done in a couple of words would be prudent.

Chapter 5:
Paid Traffic

Synopsis

Taking all the necessary steps to ensure as much traffic as possible passes through an individual's website is very important if the said individual is expecting to garner some income from the traffic visiting the site. Thus, the need to ensure the constant visits of traffic to the website.

Hits

Traffic is an ever essential tool needed for the success of any online business. When there is a lot of traffic it would mean that a lot of potential customers are being made aware of the services or precuts offered by a particular website.

However some sites can be made intentionally boring just to ensure and encourage the surfer to quickly click on the site to get out of the page as soon as possible, but to the web host the intention to get the paid traffic flow is achieved.

In terms of actually using the paid traffic method there can be advantages as well as disadvantages that need to be carefully considered.

While paid traffic is known to be able to provide the necessary means to make money it can at the same time also be a means where money is lost in huge amounts.

Perhaps the following tips should be considered before making the decision to use the paid traffic feature.

- Setting a reasonable budget to be used for the paid traffic tool would be a good start.

- Having a product that is marketable would make the paid traffic tool worth using. If the product is neither interesting nor worth considering then the paid traffic visits or hits would be of no real use.

- A certain level of staying power or patience is needed. Sometime letting the situation run its course before making any rash decision to make changes is good. Making too many changes and too often may not be beneficial; therefore a little discipline is needed.

Chapter 6:
Free Traffic

Synopsis

All businesses listed on the internet depend on free traffic to a certain extent. This free traffic facility comes with a lot of benefits and can be a value added tool for all those needing this facility to enhance their website visits.

Gratis

With the use of the free traffic system the individual gets the one way links from a huge number of real blog spots inside the vast system which is already in place.

The idea behind this tool is to try and garner the highest possible interest from the potential "hits" which jump from search engines to other links.

Here are some tips that can be used by anyone interested in getting free traffic to their web sites.

- Perhaps the first step would be to sign up for a specific free traffic account. In doing so one would be able to be linked to this site which in turn will deliberately direct traffic to the intended or listed site.

- There will probably be a need to activate the link before any activity is possible or facilitated.

- Then the individual can start designing the text required on needed to promote whatever item or service intended. This of course should be done with the precise aim of holding the attention on the potential client or customer once the connection through the free traffic is done.

- The next step would be to copy and paste the most interesting and enticing snippets to the individual's chosen site. Once this is done, then the exercise is put in motion to ensure the various systems detect and link the individual's website to as many other sites as possible. This will ensure the maximum amount to exposure possible for any posted site which in turn will garner the necessary free traffic needed to ensure the success of any site.

Chapter 7:
Using Social Media

Synopsis

In any attempt to make a success of an endeavor, the individual needs to explore all possibilities available and find the best and most suited ones to garner the necessary business income. Therefore tapping into the social media circuits can have many benefits.

A Different Way

In order to get the individual's product "recognized" posting sneak previews or feature online can be one way to go. This will garner the intended feedback necessary to perk the interest of those visiting the site.

Sharing as much connective but relevant knowledge as possible will ensure the revisits and recommended visits to one's site. This also provides other positive exposure that the potential client may not be aware of and thus create a sense of confidence and value in the company that is willing to divulge useful information for the benefit of others.

All this is done without the intention of making further money but with the intention on providing free accompanying and complimentary information.

Using the social media circuit to post as many convincing videos as possible will help the potential customer or client to be sufficiently impressed with the advertised product or service to take the next step to make either further enquiries or perhaps even a purchase.

Giving the visitor to the said site a chance to post their views or comments is another attractive way to garner the relevant interest in a website. Most people would love the opportunity to air their views on any particularly linked topic and thus by giving them the opportunity to do so; the door is opened to other interested participants too.

Being true to one's self and the contents of the website posted or hosted is definitely advisable. If there is no sincerity when using the social media style of garnering interest, then the inevitable results of not having any confidence in the site would eventually result in the redundancy of the said site.

Chapter 8:

Assembling A Team

Synopsis

The success of any endeavor depends largely on the dynamics of a successful team. When there is a good working relationship within the team makeup, the level of understanding and execution of each step of the said endeavor is done to the best of all those involved. Therein lies the importance of finding and putting together a good team.

Putting It Together

When looking for different individuals to make up a team, but without any prior knowledge of possible candidates, it would be beneficial to source these possibilities through the already known contacts even if the said contacts are not knowledgeable in the field required.

Most people already have their own network of connection that may or may not have anything to do with the particular expertise sought, but by the mere fact of having an extensive network the word is put out where possible connections can then be made.

Keeping the balance between all the different information and input by the various team members would require some sort of coordinating effort.

Thus having a central system in place where all in coming information can be formatted would help to entice potential interested parties to join the team. The potential team member would be more comfortable working in a clearly defined project style.

Money is always a lucrative way to garner interest, therefore being able to offer good remuneration for services rendered would be a good reason for those interest to consider becoming part of the team. The security offered in terms of compensation for work done would also encourage each team member to focus to ensure the entire project is successfully completed.

Keeping projects as simple as possible is another way to encourage the interest of possible candidates when trying to assemble a good workable team. If the project is easily understood and executed, the chances of being able to assemble a successful team is better.

Chapter 9:
How Important Is Customer Service

Synopsis

In today's world of ever changing technologies, products sold are becoming better and better all the time. The qualities of these products are also of a much higher standard. Therefore in order to stay competitive in the ever shrinking market share, customer service had taken on a new importance.

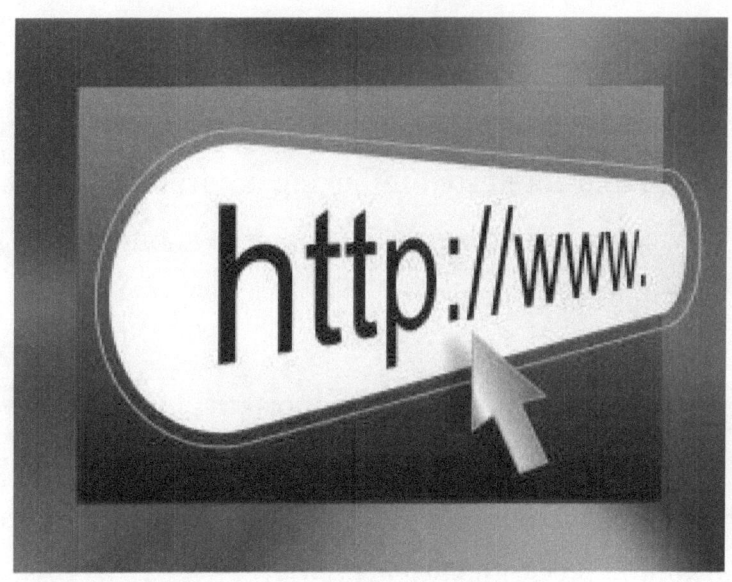

Customers

Most of the products sold today have almost if not the very same quality levels and features, thus most discerning customers are more interested in the service provided before, during and after the sale has been completed. This particular requirement has become almost as important as the product itself.

If the potential customer is not satisfied with any aspect of the service provided there is almost nothing to stop the customer from seeking the same product elsewhere. This is simply because there are always a variety of products that are available in the same category that the customer is seeking to purchase.

Proper training is also another very important feature companied need to pay attention to. The potential customer or client is not going to be impressed and interested in buying a particular product is the customer service provided is non informative enough or even worse totally and completely nonexistent.

As customer feedback is a very important tool for the further expansion and success of a company, creating good customer service modules for the hired personnel to follow is one of the prerequisites needed and should be seriously considered.

Providing good customer service would ensure the customer goes away feeling happy and satisfied with the attention and care given during the sale. This is invaluable advertising for the company as a satisfied customer is a walking and talking advert for them which is completely genuine and even more important free. Every company can benefit from this type of positive endorsement.

Chapter 10:
The Mindset Necessary For Internet Marketing Success

Synopsis

Getting carried away with promises of fast and big money is not only rather foolish but also very naive. There is no such thing as popularly advertised in the passive internet circles as making money without having to do anything. Anyone with a little common sense would be able to recognize this as virtually impossible.

Thus having unreasonable expectation on the alleged huge earnings touted would cause the individual to end up being cheated. Thus the need to be wise and well informed of every possible fact linked to the passive internet marketing tool.

Be Real

The success of the individual foray into the passive internet marketing arena very much depends on the amount or percentage the individual is able or willing to commit to the said foray. This is reflected in the mind set of the individual right from the onset of the foray into the internet marketing tool.

Also having the mindset of one who is always willing to learn of keep abreast with the latest and most innovative technologies is beneficial to creating successful passive internet marketing possibilities. When one is abreast with the latest information associated with the passive internet marketing choice then one is able to provide the best for all visitors to the said website.

Having the necessary skills needed to venture into the passive internet marketing field is advantages and it would not be wise to have to depend on other sources to provide assistance at every juncture.

Wrapping Up

Having the correct mindset in order to create a successful internet marketing foray is very important. Without the correct mind set in success of the internet marketing foray is definitely questionable.

Preparing one's self mentally is actually the biggest part and contributing factor to the ultimate success of the internet marketing foray, as well as the correct tools and knowledge.

www.ingramcontent.com/pod-product-compliance
Lightning Source LLC
Chambersburg PA
CBHW031507210526
45463CB00003B/1119